MAKING A FAMILY HOME

Making a Family Home

Shannon Honeybloom

photographs by Skip Hunt

SteinerBooks

STEINERBOOKS

An Imprint of Anthroposophic Press, Inc.

610 Main Street, Suite 1

Great Barrington, MA, 01230

www.steinerbooks.org

Cover and book design by William Jens Jensen

LIBRARY OF CONGRESS CATALOGING-IN-PUBLICATION DATA

Honeybloom, Shannon, 1969–
  Making a family home / Shannon Honeybloom ; photography
by Skip Hunt.
     p. cm.
  ISBN 978-0-88010-702-0
  1. Home economics. 2. Parenting. I. Title.
  TX301.H62 2010
  640—dc22

                                        2009038252

Contents

For my grandmother Betty Janssen Murrell,
who gave me a gift called "Home."

Acknowledgements

To Susan Howard and Ann Stahl for their encouragement and wisdom.

To William Jensen for his editorial support and beautiful design, to Winslow Eliot for her editorial suggestions, and to Christopher Bamford and Gene Gollogly for helping me bring this book forward.

To Skip Hunt for his beautiful photographs, to David Honigblum for his creative technical support and his eagle eyes, and to Candelaria for her care and kindness.

To my great aunts Dorathea and Billie, for the beautiful photos of their childhood home.

To Pat Mouton and Leslie Burchell-Fox, both wonderful teachers of young children.

To David Adams for his songs and fairy tales.

To my parents, Jane and John Wulsin, for nurturing my love of reading and writing, and Stephen and Michele Johnson for their love and interest.

To my husband Gregg, for his love, support, and patience, and for making this book possible.

To my children, Zachary, Sam, Zoe, for their love and inspiration.

And to the many others who have helped me along the way.

Introduction

What makes a house a home? A house serves as a dwelling place for one person or for a group of people. It offers shelter from the winds, the rain, snow and sleet, from hot summer sun and from cold winter nights. More than merely a dwelling, the definition of home extends beyond the meaning of a house and contains an additional poetic meaning. There's the saying, "Home is where the heart is."

Creating a home for our family can be both a challenge and a pleasure. Creating a home is a process of imbuing our space with soul and spirit, surrounding our family with love, care, comfort.

Using the insights of Waldorf education and being inspired by the works of Rudolf Steiner and others, this book opens a conversation and a dialogue about what it means to nurture young children at home and what it means to make a home for them. Pictures offer encouragement, while the text explores the many-faceted aspects of creating a home for our children.

Looking at the home, room by room, can offer inspiration and encouragement to parents seeking to nurture their families by creating a home of harmony, rhythm, and beauty.

At Home with Children

The art of homemaking and child rearing are hidden in today's culture. Many mothers, in their modern isolation from families and traditions, have lost a sense of how to care for young children and for their homes. I live more than a thousand miles away from my own mother and have been unable to rely on her daily wisdom and experience as I raise my children. Before I had children, I had never spent much time with little ones. Growing up, I hardly ever babysat. After having an overwhelming experience as a twelve-year-old babysitter, I chose to earn pocket money in other ways—by cleaning or by mowing lawns. Before I had children, I had never changed a diaper, and I barely knew how to cook. I don't think I had ever even seen a woman breastfeeding her baby.

As far as making a home...well, I had created a home just for me in a small Brooklyn apartment. But it wasn't a home that paid attention to anyone's needs except my own. When I got married, I moved into my husband's apartment. It was a fairly typical bachelor's place, with a giant TV and a state-of-the-art sound system—not necessarily a place for children.

But I wanted a baby. And pretty soon, a baby came. I did my research—bought lots of how-to books and parenting magazines and surfed the internet. I was overwhelmed. I'm not the only one. Many parents I know are overwhelmed by the wealth of information about parenting and children, and by all the responsibilities of life: work, home, children, and finances. For me, I found that paying attention to my home was (and is) a way to ground myself in the center of all the information and noise of my life. Home is the place that forms the basis for a child's future. Home is the place where children are introduced to the world. Home can help children thrive and unfold and gather courage to meet their futures.

When I was pregnant, I definitely experienced the phenomenon called "nesting." Like a mother bird, I wanted my nest, my home, to be "just right"

for my arriving baby. Lots of expectant mothers feel this way, and animals, too. Rabbits line their burrows with fur; deer prepare a hollow. Every spring the squirrels in our yard methodically rip apart our outdoor furniture cushions, seeking the choice, soft cotton for their nests.

In the middle, holding the cat is my great grandmother "Mommy" Janssen. She is holding Mickey, the beloved Persian cat. To her left is my great-great grandmother Dorathea Janssen.

My grandmother's house was an early prefab home. For many years it was painted white with green shutters, but at some point while I was growing up, my grandmother had the paint sanded off to leave the cypress wood natural.

Like the mother squirrel, I also wanted the choicest, softest cotton for my baby. I wanted to create a welcoming and health-giving environment for my children. As inspiration, I turned to memories of my grandmother and mother and the homes they created.

When my grandmother Betty died, she was seventy-eight years old. She died in the house where she was born and grew up. It was there that she raised her children, a girl and three boys. It is a cypress wood house, a two-story, center-hall colonial on the banks of Lake Martha in Winter Haven, Florida, citrus country. Built almost entirely of wood, my grandmother's home was magical for me as I grew up.

Having grown up during the Depression, my grandmother had the habit of not buying many things and fixing her things when they broke. Her home was spotless and uncluttered. Each item was carefully cleaned, placed, considered.

She created a loving home based on simplicity and modesty. It was a happy home, full of laughing children. The grandchildren constantly tracked in sand from the lake. A box of toys was kept close in a downstairs closet. A few breakable items were placed high on a mantel.

My grandmother was a teacher and a mother, a wife and a homemaker. She began raising her family in the 1940s. Her marriage was a traditional one, but she did not seem to be constrained by her homemaking duties. She was a master at making delicious, humble-looking pies slathered in meringue—

they weren't much to look at, but they were the perfect ending to a simple southern meal. The polished pinewood floors of her house shone. The white sheets with which she made all the beds were smooth and crisp. Helping her make a bed, wash the dishes, make a pie or a simple dinner, or sweep the front steps was always so much fun because of the cheerful way in which she did those household tasks. She imbued her household with love, simplicity, and joy.

My great Aunt Martha, about 1939. She was my grandmother's youngest sister.

My mother Jane playing in the front yard.

My grandmother's avocado tree.

Knut, my nephew, when he was little. Many happy children played in that yard over the years. He is in his twenties now and lives in the house.

My grandmother Betty and her three sisters, Carolyn, Billie and Dorathea. That's Mickey, the cat.

Knut, playing on the beach.

The front of the house

My grandmother Betty standing in front of her lifelong home. I remember orange trees and a giant avocado tree in the yard.

The house from the driveway

The street-side and back of the house

Although she had grown up during difficult times with little in the way of material things, she did not have the tendency to collect or accumulate. In fact, she threw away items that might have been considered precious to her children and grandchildren—her beautiful wedding dress, which she discovered years later collecting dust in the attic, was tossed without sentiment.

I grew up all over the place. I lived on a communal farm in Quincy, Florida; at an ashram in Gainesville, Florida; in a former priest's rectory in Detroit, Michigan; in a school in Denver, Colorado; and, finally, at the Threefold Community in Spring Valley, New York. Because I spent much of my early childhood wandering, my grandmother's home became for me the archetype of home.

My sister bought the house some years back. She lives there now. The home is steeped in history and family memories. My memories of the home are specific and sensory: I remember sliding down the banister, the color and feel of the banister, the incredible length of the banister, the very, very long time it took me to reach the end—my children have discovered the same joys in the banister at our house. The stairs were covered with a textured green carpet, and sand could always be flicked out of the carpet, no matter how much the vacuum had been run. The kitchen was painted yellow. In my own home I am partial to yellow walls as well, perhaps in remembrance of the yellow walls and golden light of my grandmother's home. And of course, in my memories of the home, it was enormous. As an adult, it is always a surprise to return to this place of my childhood and realize that the house is not as large as I recall.

The home in which I grew up after my initial nomadic existence, my mother's home, was completely different in style from my grandmother's home but equally filled with love, beauty, and joy. It is in Chestnut Ridge, New York, a ranch-style common to the area. My mother, her husband, and our blended family of many sisters and a brother worked together over the years to create a home that reflected us as a family.

Mementos from many travels far and wide have been added to the home over the years. It is full of Peruvian paintings, African bead work, Balinese batik cloth, homemade toy boats, shells collected from Florida beaches, crocheted blankets, paintings from second graders, handmade Valentines, and freshly baked banana bread.

My mother is nurturing and expansive. There is always an extra bed for a weary guest, plenty of food for expected and unexpected friends and impromptu parties. The garage is chock full of all manner of supplies to help the house run smoothly—extra paper towels, extra dishes culled from some garage sale, lots of canned and jarred food for emergencies and for every day.

I lived for over two years in the desert country of Niger, West Africa, as a Peace Corps volunteer. Families there create homes that are very different from ours, but still serve the same purpose: they offer shelter, a place to gather in safety, a bed on which to sleep (made of sticks and placed out under the stars). The homes usually consist of several small sleeping huts arranged around an open courtyard and surrounded by a high mud wall. Most of the living takes place outside.

When I was first married, I lived in a ground-floor apartment in New York City that looked out to a busy Second Avenue. This was the home into which I welcomed my first child. The reality of the space was that it was not a light-filled, sunlit place with birds twittering. It was dark and noisy and exposed to the smells and sights of city life. However, for me and for my new family, it was a happy, cozy, comfortable sanctuary. There are numerous different homes and living situations, and most can be made into a friendly, happy space for our family.

Many of us in North America no longer live near our parents, our grandparents, uncles, and aunts. People have moved away from their blood relations by choice or by necessity and seek a new type of family—a family or community brought together by common goals and similar ideals and ideas. Frequently, people are no longer surrounded by a traditional

familial support system and seek a new kind of support from friends and colleagues. Most North Americans move multiple times during their lifetime. They create several homes.

Creating homes is a big business. Wherever we go, we are bombarded with things that we might need for our homes. Advertisements urge us to buy, buy, buy. Magazines show us beautiful things and compel us to want these things. Stores urge us to fill our homes with all manner of useful and not-useful objects. It is never-ending, this push to buy, to accumulate, to fill our lives with things. For some, shopping has become recreational instead of need-based. For many, it fulfills the need for entertainment. In one sense, shopping is a form of hope and possibility—if I buy this scarf or that tablecloth, I will feel more beautiful and my home will be more inviting. This feeling of hope and

optimism that might accompany a purchase can also be addicting.

For many mothers, overwhelmed with the duties of homemaking and child rearing, shopping is the only time they have away from home, away from the children. Shopping provides their only legitimate break. The mothers on our block joke that a visit to the grocery store is the only time spent alone without children or spouses. All this buying has created a crisis situation for many people—enter the organizing experts and stores and more opportunities for buying in order to help us organize our things.

When I lived with my family in a New York City apartment, I was more easily able to resist the urge to buy things for my home. First of all, my space was very limited; if I added anything to my home, I really did need to remove something from it first. Also, since I was mostly on foot and did not own a car, I thought twice before purchasing something that I would have to lug home.

Moving to a home in Austin, Texas, I was initially flush with excitement at all the space I now had, and was giddy with ideas for how to fill it up with stuff. It has been a struggle for me to resist the urge to add more things to my home. One consideration that helps me curb consumer temptations is my attempt to be conscious of the affect on my children of every purchase I might make. When I have the urge to accumulate, I try to pause and make sure that the item is appropriate for them and would add to their lives in some way. I also try to find other forms of entertainment and other ways of feeling hopeful and

optimistic, such as studying and developing an artistic craft.

Home is a place that has the potential either of bringing people, friends, and family together or of thrusting them apart. It can provide an example of how one might live and work and relate outside of the home. It can also provide a basis for spiritual growth and healing.

The Senses and Other Considerations

*B*abies and children are greatly affected by their environment, completely open to the influences of the space around them. Babies live in the moment, with their senses engaged on every level. My baby loves to be touched. She relishes her body and rolls in pleasure on lambskin, delighting in the soft touch of the wool on her skin. She might pause for a moment, stretching, to notice how the light plays in a shadow, and turn toward the window at the sound of a bird.

Realizing how affected my baby was by everything happening in her presence, I wanted to make my home a place that is pleasing and comforting for her, body and soul. It also felt important to me to make my home the most healthful place possible for my children. Paying attention to the sensory experience of my baby seemed a good place to start.

Even as an adult, I know from experience that my physical surroundings affect me—the room I am in, the clothes I am wearing, the temperature, the time

of day, the quality of light, what I eat for breakfast. And babies are more vulnerable to their surroundings and defenseless than adults are.

Increasingly, children and adults are experiencing disorders in relation to their senses. One of my sons was very particular about his clothing as a toddler. Clothing bothered

him unless it was very loose, and it had to be blue. My other son chews on his shirt constantly. I can't stand the texture of certain foods and am over-stimulated and irritable in crowds. My niece is going through a stage in which she will eat only crunchy food. My friend's child refuses to wear anything with a button on it. My colleague can hardly speak in a restaurant if there is any background music. A lot of people can't stand the scratch of chalk on a chalkboard. Many people I know must deal with some sort of sensory-related issue. That is one reason that the sensory environment of the home is so important. If the home can nurture the senses, and even be healing to our senses, our children are all the more well-equipped for school and to go out into the world with fewer sensory issues.

What we experience with our senses affects our emotions. Even in language we adapt sensory expressions to describe our feelings. We say things like: She's "touchy." He's "abrasive." We are "hot and bothered" or "cool and calm." An unfortunate experience leaves a "bad taste." Someone might be in a "sour" mood or another might be characterized as "sweet." When we understand something, we might say, "I see!" Our bodies and the experience of our senses are integrated with our emotional well-being.

The twelve senses and their relation to the home are helpful to consider as we create homes for our children:

1. Touch—the experience of the skin meeting whatever is just beyond it—soft, hard, smooth or bumpy, the pleasure of a warm hug or the pain of falling down on a rock. Touch gives us the experience of the boundaries of our bodies.

2. Life sense—the feeling of being well or of feeling ill, being hungry or full, in pain or contented.

3. Self-movement—gestures, walking or crawling, reaching and holding, the ability to be free in our movement, and the realization of the limits of our movement.

4. Balance—a child learns to balance, stand, and walk. When our balance is out of whack, we become dizzy and feel sick.
5. Smell—odors attract or repel.
6. Taste—our tongues can distinguish tastes that are tart, salty, sweet, soapy, sour, and bitter.
7. Vision—our eyes can perceive shape and color, light and shadow.
8. Temperature—our bodies can feel warm or cold.
9. Hearing—we have the capacity to perceive sound.
10. Language sense—we learn to understand language, speech.
11. Conceptual sense—we can develop the ability to perceive the meaning of a word or concept.
12. "I" sense—we have the ability to recognize our self as separate from the self of another person.

The domestic arts—cooking, baking, cleaning, making, and so on—are central aspects to creating a living, artistic home atmosphere. Natural materials—wood, stone, cotton, wool, silk—help to keep children (and adults) in touch with nature and natural processes. Attention and consciousness toward our inner life keeps us striving as individuals. This private struggle informs and encourages our children and manifests in the care we take in organizing our surroundings.

Technology, both useful and superfluous, pervades and even dominates many aspects of our lives, including our lives at home. From the vacuum to the computer, from the toaster to the television, we incorporate technology and its effects into our lives. We can use technology in a thoughtful and conscious manner.

We can feel the difference upon entering a space that has been worked with and consciously considered, in contrast to a space that has been put together with little attention. In putting together my own home, I have tried to do so deliberately, asking myself the questions: What makes a space sheltering, harmonious, and healthy? What kinds of materials can be used in building and furnishing my home that can help in the development of my children?

Aesthetic considerations are an important part of homemaking. I try to surround my children with beauty and harmony, and I feel that this can have a therapeutic effect—an antidote to the dusky, grey, concrete experiences of our streets, cities, and suburbs. Making a home also reaches past aesthetic and utilitarian considerations, expanding to include personal meaning and self-expression, emotional connection, memories of the past and hopes for the future.

The Front Porch

The front porch extends the house into the yard. It is an inside/outside transition space. The front porch is a welcoming space, a space of meeting, greeting, leaving, and transition. Front porches draw the inhabitants of the house outside, bring neighbors into conversation with one another, ease social isolation, and provide a public space of respite, shelter, and shade.

I live in an older neighborhood with homes built on small lots in the early part of the 1900s. Our street has sidewalks where children play, ride bikes, jump hopscotch, and sell lemonade, where neighbors gather. None of the homes have attached garages, and this encourages neighbors to engage with one another before entering their homes, fostering a sense of community. Some of the homes have a front porch, or at least some sort of front yard sitting area—a place to be sheltered from the bright sun while watching the children play, a comfortable place from which to watch the day go by.

In what may be a sign of our increasing social isolation, many homes built today do not have a front porch or scarcely any public seating and greeting area. Many of us find that we are turned inward—inward in the home, further inward sitting at the computer or the TV. Reclaiming a front porch, or creating a front porch area, can

be one way which we can reach out to our neighbors and friends.

Our home does not have a front porch, but we have created a front-porch area out front by placing a bench in our yard and hanging a swing bench from a tree. Both swing and bench are wonderful places from which to watch the children play and catch up with the neighbors. We also nailed slats to our big front yard oak tree—the children love to climb on it, and survey the neighborhood from the arms of the tree. These two things—the swing bench and making the tree more accessible—have greatly increased our use of the front yard.

I try to reach out to my neighbors and to my community—by offering meals during stressful times or through a simple wave and a smile across the lawn. Forging human connections, creating emotional and spiritual bonds with others, is important for individual happiness and growth. Being sometimes shy, I feel lucky that my children are so excellent at making friends. Through my children, I have met many people I otherwise would not have met. The challenges of parenting are compounded by the solitary lives we lead: seek community and conversation for support and companionship.

It is true that most of us do not live on Main Street, USA, where happy people are waving and beckoning from their front doors. Many suburban neighborhoods are isolated on the fringes of a highway, and the living situation can be reclusive and antisocial. Especially in these situations, the front porch can be extended to include the neighborhood coffee shop, deli, bagel store, coop—making regular visits to local institutions and community gathering places and fostering relationships with the people we encounter in these places eases the isolation of modern living.

Once I was visiting a friend, and we stopped by the gas station to fill up her car. We walked into the station to pay, and she knew and greeted everybody there. Afterward, she told me that she considers the exchange of money an opportunity to make a connection with another human being. I have tried to follow her example in my own life, using the exchange of money as a moment and opportunity to connect.

When I lived in Africa, I became used to a very social type of living. People spent all day and night surrounded by others, parenting groups of children together, sharing meals together. And on the streets and in the marketplace, everyone always said hello— sometimes it took a very long time to get from one place to another because the constant acts of greeting were so extensive and inclusive! When I returned after two and a half years there, I experienced a little reverse culture shock—it hurt me that everyone was not saying hi to each other, and that some people would even avert their eyes and hurry away, avoiding human contact. My first job in New York City was at an office with a lot of cubicles. I was working as a grants writer for a nonprofit organization and found myself glued to my computer, and when I wasn't glued to my computer, I was taking a break on the city streets, where everyone avoided eye contact. Even though I was surrounded by people, I felt lonely.

Now, back in the U.S. for many years, I find that much of my time is spent alone, with just my children or my husband. It is an effort to include others into my routines. Caring for my children solo, I am often overwhelmed. I am always happy when the grandparents come to visit, and I realize that parenting is so much more rewarding when it takes place within a community, a larger context. I know that there are many women who spend the early parenting years feeling incredibly alone, and it is not until the children reach school age that some parents find a community within which to raise their children, if even then.

Children and adults have the opportunity to forge connections with others in the front yard, at the entrance to their homes. Most children are naturally outgoing. My children love to engage with the neighbors and other children, to see the mail carrier and the garbage collector. Children love to see action and work. Witnessing work stimulates their abilities and capacities.

Increasingly, children are kept inside—at the computer, at the TV, playing video games. For fear of broken bones, kidnapping, car accidents, and so on, children are kept inside, "safe." It is true that the home should be a safe place, a sanctuary, but also we can help our children see the world outside the home as a good place, as a place to play and to explore without fear.

Many mothers are not comfortable allowing their children to walk to school unattended or to roam and play in the neighborhood without constant supervision. We have all heard the horror stories of abducted children. It seems as if we hear of tragedies every day. As a child, I remember wandering the neighborhood on bikes and on foot, exploring field, stream, back alleys, garages, ponds, woods—all manner of places, without direct adult supervision. This helped me to trust the world around me. Many of our children today are not learning to trust, but to mistrust and to fear. While some of this fear may be grounded, extreme behavior and imbalanced behavior is not healthy for us as parents or for our children. For me, having children has been (and continues to be) a lesson in learning how to let go of many of my fears.

A front porch is also a place of shelter for those about to enter into the home as well as a place of safety for those stepping outside. One of the first things I do every morning is step outside onto our front steps to check the weather and greet the day. My children are usually right there with me, also ready to go outside after the night.

The Front Door, the Entryway

The front door provides a way into our homes. The front door welcomes home our family and welcomes our guests into our homes. Entering the doorway into a home is essentially a threshold experience, of being on the brink between inside and outside. This experience happens many times during the day. One leaves the outside, one arrives inside; a transformation takes place. We can be transformed by the simple act of entering a home. For children, entering their own home can be a magical moment. A child enters a place of shelter, safety, and security.

In the temples and cathedrals of old, doorways were often splendid arches, soaring high, welcoming one inside, and inviting a person into a particular experience. It is not uncommon today for many houses to contain arches at the front door in some form—the arch of an adobe house, the wooden arch of a craftsman bungalow. An arch is often built between the rooms themselves.

All forms impress deeply upon a young child. The experience of an arch between the threshold of inside or outside, between the various

and worked with by the front door, extending into the front yard. We plant bulbs to welcome the spring; in summertime the flowers bloom in our front yard beds; in autumn the bright pumpkins and gourds arrive; in winter we build snowmen and scrape the snow from our door so that it remains accessible to family and friends.

A front walkway of stone or cement is surrounded by the grass and plants of the front yard, a front step of stone or wood, a front door of wood or metal. In this way, the elements of nature are included in our welcoming space. The front door

rooms throughout a home, offers a contrast to the straight walls and rigid corners of the conventional room. Children love the fluidity of curve and circle. The arch of an entrance can be a way to recognize and work with this experience.

A front door trellis is another arch that can be incorporated into a home or garden. It confirms and extends further the indoor/outdoor threshold.

The front door represents a space that is both inside and outside, a transition. Seasons of the year are often acknowledged

to every practical detail, is a form of love that gives the home its warmth.

Any entrance room can provide a way to work with the transition from outside to inside—a small bench provided for taking off boots or a table for placing one's keys and the mail, a basket or shelf for shoes. It is a space that can be used to echo the outside. Traditionally a bouquet of flowers is often placed in the entryway. A crystal, a basket of shells can be placed in this space to provide transition from outside to inside and to welcome the elements into our home.

A mudroom facilitates the transition between the indoors and the outdoors. It has hooks for coats and baskets or cubbies for boots and shoes, gloves, and hats. Even in a home without a specific mudroom (our home in Texas doesn't have one), practical elements can be incorporated. We have a basket by the door for shoes, another basket to capture keys and mail, a closet for coats and sweaters, and a mat by the door to wipe the dust off our feet.

In some cultures, removing one's shoes indoors is the normal practice. It is something to consider—in our New York City apartment, keeping the soot of the city at bay was nearly impossible, and taking our shoes off at the door seemed a necessity. In Austin, where we are in and out of the house continually all day long, we are less likely to remove our shoes every time we enter our home (or to put them on each time we leave).

can invite the elements into our homes by acknowledging them and working with them in a conscious way.

Opening our door, we are provided with our first glimpse into the home. Some may have an entrance that provides hints of outdoor life—the coat closet, hat racks, scarves and mittens in a basket. The outer life is put away in this room, in preparation for the inner life of the home. This attention to function in each room,

One of the first things one notices when entering a home is the smell. We open the door, step in, and take a deep breath, noticing the smell of the space. A clean fresh smell is certainly most inviting—whether the smell of flowers, the smell of baking, or the fresh smell of herbs or fruit. The sense of smell gives us an immediate indication of the kind of space we are entering.

Smell comes upon us invisibly. Sometimes a smell has the power to send us back to our own childhood—to the green fresh smell of the bushes by the front door, mother's cookies baking, the scents of climbing the pine tree in the back yard.

In paying attention to the smells of our own home, we are developing the child's sense of smell. I try to avoid smells that are too strong, chemically based, or toxic. The gentle smells of baking, of cleaning with nontoxic solutions, of aromatherapy, of the spring breeze coming in from the window, can delicately welcome us home.

The threshold of the home is a place of transition and a place of welcoming. It is the place of greeting. It can be a place where we can leave what might be cold and frightening outside as we enter the warmth and comfort of the home.

The Living Room

From the threshold of the front door, we enter the living room. The living room is a space for family life, social arts, and indoor play. It is often the location of the hearth, symbolizing the warmth and spirit of the home.

The living room is a place for the family to interact. Human contact and relationships bring warmth and love to our lives. Involvement with others enriches our lives. The home is the place where children, indeed each of us, learn to love. The homemaker has a significant task in nurturing the ability to love among the children and family members.

Love is a growing, developing process. The Greeks had terms for several kinds of love that can be experienced and can build upon one another:

Eros—physical, passionate identification;

Philia—love of the soul, friendship, heartfelt;

Storge—love of mothers for their children, deep, overflowing, permanent;

Agape—mutual moral warmth, respect, sacrifice.

Home is a place where many levels of love manifest. For example, physical love (*eros*) helped provide the spark and the initial attraction that brought our children to us.

On the level of the soul (*philia*), the harmony with which we are able to manage the various personalities of the household is a form of love. The warm, heartfelt friendship that we extend to our family members and beyond—this is also love.

The love I have for my children as a mother (*storge*) nourishes and supports them. This love, continuous and protective, I express through smoothing my son's hair before sending him off to school, taking my daughter into my lap to read a story, and kissing my son before bed.

Spiritual love (*agape*)—recognition, esteem, and sacrifice—is the most powerful form of love we can offer. Cultivating deep, moral warmth for another, filled with respect and with the willingness to sacrifice, is the most challenging kind of love that we can strive to give to those around us.

Family life gives us the opportunity to learn and to teach all these levels of love. If within our homes we can learn to love, this love can provide a basis for transformation within our families and in the world beyond. In addition to the physical, the home can be considered the spiritual center of a child's experiences.

In creating our homes, we can nurture these kinds of love and find them present in everything that we do. Caring for the physical comfort of others, providing shelter from the elements, is an act of love. If we can be comfortable and happy in our bodies, if we feel well cared for, then we have the ability to turn our attention to our life's work. If our bodies are provided for and at ease, then our souls and spirits can be free to attend to other concerns. If our relationships are harmonious, our emotions steady, our soul-life even and fulfilled, we are happy. If our spirit is engaged, if we are striving to help others and to understand the world around us, then we can be at peace in the world.

On the physical level, it is increasingly the case that adults and children are not at ease in their physical bodies. All sorts of sensory disorders and imbalances manifest in us and in our children.

I struggle with being at ease in my own body—feeling awkward, uncomfortable in my skin. This difficulty extends into my emotional life, making me at times shy, reticent, and sensitive. One of my children faces a similar challenge. However, through conscious touch (the nightly massage, lots of hugs), through hard pressure experiences (roughhousing,

trampoline jumping), we are working on bringing him into balance, and I am learning lots about my own limitations and difficulties in the process. Home can be a therapeutic place that helps us overcome our sensory difficulties.

The home is where one develops or experiences sympathy and antipathy toward family members and guests, toward all who enter the home. Sympathies warm the soul; antipathies chill the soul. Both present an extreme that is balanced by empathy. Homemakers can nurture empathy in the home through their qualities of listening and through interest. Interest itself can be a form of love. Listening, putting away our own judgment, cares, and concerns in order to see the other is also a form of love.

Listening and hearing require us to be still inside, to silence any inner dialogue and temporarily give up our own cares to really hear the other. Listening to another

is a way to give love to another. Love can be thought of as the ability to truly hear the other. Children are begging to be heard and seen—tugging at the sleeve of the parent, screaming for attention, turning the distracted parent's face toward their own: Listen to me. Look at me.

The homemaker, the mother or the father, is in a unique position to practice and foster love in the home and beyond. Simple considerations can help homemakers. For example, the arrangement of the living room and the use of the room can encourage empathy, interest, love. Comfortable seating can be arranged in the living room so as to encourage conversation and contact among family members and guests. Chairs and sofas arranged in a kind of circle encourage more interaction than lining up all the furniture against the wall. A reading corner with a comfortable chair and good lighting will encourage reflection.

Some baskets of toys in a corner of the room will provide something for the children to do while the adults are engaged in conversation or other matters. Young children spend an enormous amount of time at home. A happy healthy home can provide a lifetime of security and warmth, helping the children in their capacity to love. Each room of the home can have elements in it that include and remember the child. By having some toys and a soft blanket, the living room can be a place for the whole family to come together with

individual tasks and occupations.

The living room is often the place in the home where, in addition to the basket of toys, there are a TV, a DVD player, a computer with internet access and with downloaded computer games, iPods and iPod stereo speakers, Xboxes, and other assorted electronic toys and playthings. Ideally, the computer and other electronics could be kept elsewhere, away from spaces used frequently by the children.

Although various forms of media and all sorts of electronic stimulus have become a part of daily life for many, they do not support the healthy development of children.

When my first child was a toddler, I could not figure out how to take a shower and keep him busy while I did so. So I sat him in front of the TV, found some sort of child-centered show, and retreated by myself to the bathroom for a break. However, after doing this for a little while, I became aware of several things. First, he seemed "catatonic" in front of the TV, and it was disturbing to see him in that state. When I turned it off, he would act like an addict being denied his fix—a tantrum at worst, whining at best. Then, for days he would be trapped uncontrollably in replaying whatever he had witnessed on the television, trying to digest the experience and play out the various characters. His own imaginative play became limited. For hours on end, he could "be" only some particular television character. I might get my fifteen-minute shower break, but I was paying the price in having to manage his moodiness and wild play afterward.

So I stopped it cold turkey and found other ways of entertaining him while I showered—some toys on the bathroom floor and singing in the shower often worked. Though he was initially disappointed at being denied his television program, and I initially missed my electronic babysitter, I was amazed at how much more harmonious and healthy my son seemed without the influence of the television.

I have the same experience myself when I watch TV. I am glazed-eyed and motionless while watching, and afterward, I am restless and over-stimulated and exhausted at the same time.

Like junk food, the images on TV provide titillation without any real nourishment. In the same way that one can eat delicious, junky potato chips by the bag or glazed doughnut holes one after the other—and still be hungry because the body has not received any nourishment—the images on TV are enticing as the eyes seek real experiences to watch. Because no real experience is being witnessed, only the patterned flickering of lights, the eyes and soul remain hungry and tempted to binge until real nourishment is received. In my experience, televisions, computers, and electronic playthings are not helpful for children.

A living room can encourage the coming together of all members of the family, with space remaining for possible guests. It can be a place of warmth and relaxation, as well as of industry and occupation. Lighting, both bright and dim, can be offered.

It makes sense to seek comfortable couches, cushions, chairs, textures. A variety of seating possibilities can be offered—some for lounging after a difficult day when the bones are aching, some for sitting alert during an engaging conversation. In a sense, the home is an offering to both ourselves and our friends. We can honor ourselves and each other by seeking to provide harmony and comfort within our homes.

Warm colors—natural wood, yellows, reds—can instill a feeling of warmth and community, as opposed to fluorescent lighting and unfriendly starkness. A lot of institutional architecture—airports, hospitals, motels, prisons—strikes me as lacking any real warmth. Designed with a strictly utilitarian or pragmatic approach, they often do not have a personal, individual touch. A home is different; it is soulful and reflective of the homemaker and family and can be intensely personal.

Not just warm colors, but also colors in the cool spectrum have their place, especially in well-lit rooms with plenty of natural sunlight to provide warmth. Blues and Greens, the colors of lakes and oceans, can feel refreshing and soothing.

Sunlight shining through the window, catching a crystal hanging there and flooding the room with rainbows, is magical for children and adults alike.

Welcoming and comfortable, the living room can provide the family an inner respite from the activities of the outer world. The living room is a place for family activities. We like to read together, curled up on the couch, play games, sing songs. Some afternoons a table is covered with crafts projects and the children are busy at work. Some evenings we sit comfortably reading before heading upstairs to bed. The living room is a place for us to share the excitement of the day through conversation, as well as a place to relax during quiet, intimate moments.

The Fireplace

The fireplace, the hearth, generally has a place in a living room, providing warmth to the home. The spirit of the house could be said to reside in the hearth. The fireplace in older times was the place of warmth and light in the home. An actual fireplace is not always needed or available in a home, and that's fine. We can think of it symbolically as the soul of the home: it is the place from which warmth and feeling emanate.

Spiritual and emotional warmth can shape the atmosphere of the room, making it a place of ease and comfort. The home as a whole provides a shield of physical warmth, in addition to a fire, a heating system, or warm clothing of natural fibers. It also shelters us from the weather and wind outside.

Light and warmth are two important aspects of home life. The warmth and light of a fire as we come in from the cold and darkness give us a sense of safety, nourishment, and comfort. Warmth is expressed by the human soul as interest, inclusion, attention, absorption, enthusiasm. A child hopes to be met with warmth, both spiritual and physical—the love of a mother toward the little one, which she radiates while holding the child in her arms.

Another sensory challenge facing young children is the inability to determine if they are warm or cold. It is up to the parents to determine whether a child is appropriately dressed for the weather. My children seem to resist any sort of "extra" clothing. We struggle to find a way to keep them comfortable—clothing tags not itching, sleeves not too tight, while at the same time keeping them warm. Preserving warmth is important for both children and adults.

These days, we often experience light within the home by flicking a switch and experience warmth by turning up the heat. A fire in the hearth, however, provides an experience of light and heat that can be more immediate and striking.

The fireplace is a magical place for children and adults alike. Santa Claus comes down the chimney with his generous gifts. Storks bring babies to chimneys. In some cultures it is considered good luck to see a chimney sweep.

Warmth is important for developing children. The life forces of growing children

need warmth and light in order to thrive. Inner light and warmth nourish those who live in the home. The light and warmth of humor and laughter, of devotion and piety, affect the home deeply. The ability to laugh at our cares and sorrows elevates the mood of the home and nourishes life at home. Respect, awe and interest in the world nourish as well.

We talk of "feeling warm inside" when we think of someone we love. When describing someone who is devastatingly attractive, we might use the word "hot." If we "warm up to something," we feel enthusiasm. In language and in experience, warmth and love are interconnected.

Warmth is also essential for healthy growth and physical development. We can see this by considering geography—in the warmer climates, plants and animals flourish and expand and grow. In colder parts of the earth, or during colder parts of the year, plants contract back into the earth or die and the trees lose their leaves. Children are growing and forming their limbs and organs. It is healthy for children to be warmly dressed during the day and warmly covered at night when they sleep.

In traditional times, mothers kept a basket of work and craft projects near the hearth. One can imagine mothers of an earlier time, knitting by the fire, sewing shirts, darning socks. Sewing, knitting, making clothes and necessities were once considered essential life skills. Today we do not need to make our clothing, build our shelter, and cook our own food.

Our busy lives prohibit us from making things. If a new scarf is needed, off we go to a big-box shopping mecca or to a local clothing store. However, if time or interest permits, it can be helpful to our home-making to take up a new craft or domestic skill. Making things for one's family nurtures the qualities of self-sustainability, creativity, inspiration, and confidence.

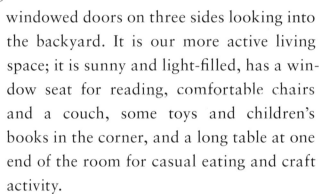

My son learned to knit in the first grade at school. He loves it. Many evenings before bed he knits the evening away with busy fingers. And I love the treasures that he makes—the pouches and the little stuffed chickens.

Handmade items are generally more valued than their machine-made counterparts. People intuit that the maker of an object pours his or her spirit and vitality into the work. The aspect of true handwork enlivens a home, and the object itself acquires something of the soul forces of the maker. We can create many things for the home—for ornamentation as well as for use. We can be conscious creators instead of consumers.

Essentially, our own home has two living rooms—one in the back of the house with

windowed doors on three sides looking into the backyard. It is our more active living space; it is sunny and light-filled, has a window seat for reading, comfortable chairs and a couch, some toys and children's books in the corner, and a long table at one end of the room for casual eating and craft activity.

Our other living room we think of as sort of a library room. It is in the front of the

house, in the original part of the home, built in the 1930s. The windows are

smaller here and the room has more shadows and darkness. This room has a fireplace. It is an intimate and cozy room and it lends itself to intimate and cozy activities. The walls of the room are lined with books, making it a good place to curl up with one in front of a flickering fire. Our hearth room is a quiet space, good for an afternoon siesta. The gentle shadows also offer a cool respite from sunny, hot, bright Austin days.

The Playroom

S ome homes have a space that can be given over to children, to their activities and playthings. We have a playroom that is furnished simply with some shelves and a daybed. On the shelves we have arranged the toys by type into small baskets. On the window sill, a small collection of wool finger puppets stand ready for play.

Against the wall is a daybed covered by a comfortable lambskin along with some pillows under a draped muslin canopy, which can be open or closed. This is a favorite spot for the children; they lie on the lambskin with a book, or they close the muslin drapes around themselves to create a little fort, a castle, a tee-pee, or a knight's tent.

A closet in this room is the perfect place to hang dress-up clothes and organize costumes.

Parents know how easy it is to accumulate stuff for children. In preparation for the birth of my first child, I collected an enormous amount of equipment (in my tiny apartment) to care for the little baby. Well-meaning

grandparents, uncles and aunts, and family friends constantly shower children with toys. Many of my relatives do not have the same ideas about child development that I do, and the toys they bring—computerized, plastic, noisy, flashy—are not the kind of toys I feel to be healthy for my children. Those toys are, however, the best and most exciting toys the giver has experienced and are given with real joy and love. I do understand the gift giver's desire to buy the most wonderful toy, and for some this means an elaborate and complicated toy.

Gentle conversations with my family and friends have helped somewhat. I also provide them with catalogues and websites and specific suggestions for gifts. Some of the best toys do not need to be purchased—they can be found or made. The stick is one of the most popular toys in our family and in our neighborhood. It is also widely available and comes in a variety of lengths and thicknesses. There are many uses for a stick—as a drilling tool, as a magic wand, as a building component, a little man.

I have noticed that toys in which everything is already complete and detailed (such as muscular and rigid action figures) have no room left over for the imagination. Such toys are so defined that they offers little in the way of flexibility. These types of toys are often quickly abandoned. Undefined toys, on the other hand, like sticks, can be many things at different moments.

Dolls that have one expression molded, painted, or sewn into them have only the single emotion defined by its detailed expression. A doll whose face is less defined, gives children more freedom to imagine what the doll might be feeling at any given time, and that feeling can change to be true to whatever situation the child's imagination has conjured.

As parents, we are also responsible for the aesthetic experience of our children. Many toys on the shelves of toy stores, when considered objectively, offer little in the way of aesthetic value; the colors are strange, the shapes are inorganic, the noises are harsh and jarring.

We need to offer our children all kinds of play opportunities and a variety of rhythmical activities to help them grow up happy and healthy.

The Kitchen

The kitchen, which traditionally contained the hearth for cooking and warmth, is often considered the heart of the home. It is a place of nourishing, a place of gathering and cooking, a place of work and creation. Activities in the kitchen are rhythmical and transformative. Cooking is a transformation through warmth. The rhythms of the day are marked in the kitchen by the creation of meals.

Cooking transforms food. Through warmth and fire, through cutting and shaping, through human activity, nourishment is created for the family. Parents can imbue their food with soul and spiritual warmth through their intentions during the process of cooking and presenting and giving the meal to their families.

In our search for health and wellness and youth and beauty, we are particularly susceptible to food fads and eating trends. It is helpful to have a few guidelines to help in our food choices. Eating local food is an important consideration; by eating locally raised food, we are eating in harmony with the season, as well as supporting and connecting with local growers.

If a food is highly processed, it is essentially predigested, requiring little from the body for assimilation. If the body is not challenged during the digestion process, then it isn't strengthened either. Whole grains, hearty breads, fruits, and vegetables are part of an ideal diet.

Refined sugar is best kept for special occasions. When I eat refined sugar, I crave more of it, and then it makes me a little nervous and edgy, and after a bit I crash and feel moody. My children are even more sensitive to sugar than I am, and I try to limit how much refined sugar they eat. Of course, we all need a little sweetness in our lives, but instead of using refined sugar, we can eat fruit, or sweeten up a recipe with honey or maple syrup.

Cooking has almost become a lost art. Prepackaged, ready-made food is often the norm in even the most thoughtful and conscious of households. My grandmother was a master of the pie crust. She would never have dreamed of using a store-bought crust—it is so simple, after all, to make pie crust: some flour, some water, some butter. But with three children at my feet, and feeling sometimes overwhelmed and lost in my responsibilities and under-confident in my abilities, I am tempted to pick up that store-bought

crust. And sometimes I do. Packaged, processed foods and machine-made meals offer a tempting shortcut. I try to resist.

Planning a rhythmical weekly menu has been very helpful for me in nourishing my family. For a while, each child was insisting on a specific meal, every meal—one wanted oatmeal for breakfast, the other a bagel. One wanted quesadillas for dinner, the other wanted broccoli and pasta shells. Now we have oatmeal on Monday mornings. On Tuesday nights, we have a Mexican-themed dinner. Each night has some sort of theme around which to build a meal. I no longer cook different meals for each child, and every week the children look forward with security to their favorite meals as they make their weekly appearance.

Of course, we don't always adhere to our schedule, and have lapsed entirely at times in favor of more spontaneous creations. However, when I am feeling at a loss as to how to feed my children nutritious meals, I have found that it helps to

turn to the schedule for guidance and inspiration. Of course, we still have our mealtime challenges. My middle child is a very picky eater. I don't battle him—his stomach is very sensitive, and he has sensory issues with certain food textures and tastes—me, too; I can't stand the texture of beef, for example, or the rubbery feel of a mushroom in the mouth. I try to be understanding and offer him possibilities and opportunities to expand his taste buds without turning mealtimes into a power struggle.

Children love to participate in cooking for the family. The kitchen is a place for children to create and work. Through activities that engage the physical world and require children to be physically active (like cooking or planting flowers), children learn to love what is good in the world. Parents can also engage their own will, their own resolve, with awareness in their work, carefully considering all thoughts and actions and words so that what they do reiterates for their children that the world is good.

Activities that engage the will—a person's ability to act and to do things, to

make things happen—might include such work as cooking, sawing, cutting, and cleaning. The kitchen is a wonderful place for children to experience real and useful work: making a snack, washing the dishes. A demeanor of thankfulness and gratitude can be fostered in children through their hard work. Other activities that strengthen the will include emphasizing the rhythms of the day, the week, the month, and the year (for example, through bedtime routines, Sunday pancakes, birthday celebrations).

Cooking is also an artistic activity. The arts and culture have important places within the home. Artistic activities can be spiritually inspired and elevate a home. A child drawing, a mother sewing or singing, making music, modeling, and

painting can nourish the members of a household. These activities nourish the soul and they speak to a love of beauty. Through artistic activity, physical things or physical actions can become beautiful. Artistic activities such as music, speech, puppetry, stories, and circle games develop a sense of beauty and a love of beauty. These activities bring harmony and friendship to children.

Many work activities are artistic—as in the term *domestic arts*. Household duties not only educate the will, but also nourish the soul if they are taken up in an artistic manner. A clean and polished floor is a work of art; sweeping a floor can be a beautiful dance and result in an ordered and artistic experience, both in the process and in the result. If good work is raised into the sphere of the beautiful, it becomes an art.

Just as cooking is the penetration of matter by a human being, so, too, is cleaning. Cleaning is an activity for the entire home and happens especially often in kitchens. Though most of us have the assistance of a vacuum cleaner and a dishwasher, whereby the push of a button enables the work to be done, brooms and damp cloths remain a part of our everyday cleaning experience. By going through space and matter, cleaning, we participate in a process that releases the dirt and weight of the physical world, allowing a lighter, more spacious element to enter the home.

A home that has not been cleaned can feel constricted and suffocating. When my home is freshly clean, I have the sensation of being able to breathe. A home that has been thoroughly scrubbed gives me a certain feeling of being liberated. De-cluttering experts talk about how "a weight is lifted" through the process of de-cluttering. I know that feeling.

Some of the happy moments from my childhood are of cleaning house and washing dishes with my mother. It was a time when we could be together, in literal harmony, both with our singing and with our hands at work. It was a time when we could experience positive and immediate results from our efforts. Cleaning can give instant results. It can quickly change the mood and feel of a space, as well as the mood and the feelings of the participants.

Sometimes when I am tired and rushed, I look at the mess my three children have made in the house through their exuberant play. And when it is time to straighten things, I am not always patient and kind. But during those times I try to remember what a happy and rewarding time cleaning up can be, and I try to change my mood in order to offer that kind of experience to my children. My children do enjoy straightening a room (most of the

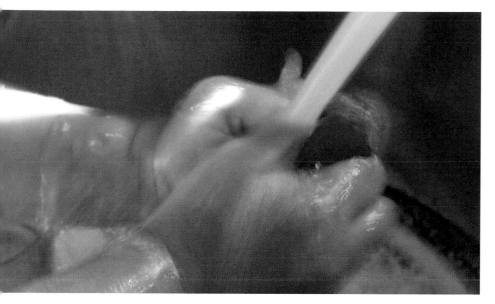

time, and especially if I am helping them), and they love to clean with water—mopping and window washing are particular favorites. We have had to invest in several mops, so that all the children can be happily working together.

Cleaning is a process of maintaining, touching. It is a process of caring, of paying attention to our surroundings and our relationships. Just as we show our children love, respect, attention, cleaning also provides us an opportunity to show this same care to our surroundings.

Many commonly available cleaning products are toxic and unfriendly, both to the environment and to us. After I had children, I became much more conscious of the cleaning products I use in my home, rejecting the highly chemical products that are so readily available. I have pared down my cleaning supplies significantly. Water is the most important ingredient for house cleaning and is sometimes all that is needed for mopping, dusting, and washing. I also use a natural soap such as Dr. Bronner's soap when needed. I add essential oils, chosen for their scent as well as their anti-bacterial and anti-viral qualities, to a water base. Lavender oil is a good choice for cleaning, as well as the oils of lemon, eucalyptus, tea tree, peppermint. Baking Soda is good for scouring. White vinegar is good for washing windows.

Homemakers are concerned with the thinking, feeling, and willing aspects of the household. Cleaning offers an opportunity to work with these three qualities; it is a process that can help us bring order to our thoughts (thinking), affect the mood of our home (feeling), and bring us into activity (willing).

The Dining Room

Mealtimes offer families and friends an opportunity to gather together, to be with each other. In the dining room, the presentation and sharing of meals offer opportunities to express our love for one another. The attention paid to the presentation of the meal—the carefully placed plate, the lovingly folded napkin, the bouquet of flowers at the table—shows love and respect for our guests and family and for the food we share. What we see with our eyes can nourish us. This makes the presentation of the meal important—a table that is set in a pleasing and orderly manner, a place mat set with care under the plate, is beneficial to our senses. It is a way to honor those at the table and a way to give thanks for the meal received.

The tradition of breaking bread together, of sharing a meal, helps in community building. In these busy days of unceasing distractions, mealtimes can be a moment to pause in our day, to come together and converse. In present times of endless interruptions and diversions, a meal is

an opportunity to share food, life, love, laughter, tears. It also offers the family a sense of rhythm in a day that otherwise may be chaotic and disjointed. Rhythm in turn offers children a sense of security and well being.

A meal can be an opportunity for healing through rhythm, nourishment, and sharing. A meal is an important social activity. Families gather to share a meal and to connect with one another. At times, it can be difficult to gather for a meal, requiring an extra force of determination and cooperation to bring everyone together.

In addition to our daily meals together, celebrations also take place around a meal. Parties and celebrations can be oppor-

tunities to mark the special moments in the year and in our lives, candles are lit and crystal is polished. A holiday celebration marks a certain time of year and a certain occasion; often extended family and friends are brought together to mark the occasion. These celebrations can be

very important for the young child. They acknowledge in an outward celebration what a child is experiencing inside—the change of the seasons, for example, or the excitement of turning a year older. The child feels recognized by the world.

Festivals are important for children and for the family. Many of us today feel isolated and alone—our work may be solitary, our motherhood lonely. Festivals help to alleviate some of that solitude.

When I had my first child, I had never felt lonelier. Suddenly I was no longer working, thereby losing the social companionship of the workplace. It was difficult to leave the house, what with nap schedules, inhospitable weather, discomfort and unfamiliarity with public breast-feeding, and all the equipment of babyhood—strollers, diapers, and wipes. I was completely in love with my baby, yet completely alone and even helpless as a new mother.

Motherhood can be an intensely isolating experience. The needs of our babies and children generally take precedence over everything else—the diaper must be changed, the baby must nap and be fed. Our own needs and desires are by necessity often placed on the back burner. It took time to figure out how to get out into the world again as mother and baby.

Festivals, both personal and cultural, are opportunities for gathering people together, offering support and friendship to each other. Fear, doubt, and anger sometimes pervade our days and nights. We are bombarded by news from the radio, the internet, the TV, newspapers, and magazines, and more often than not the news is tragic. Bringing people together for a festival is an opportunity to foster warmth, hope, and love within our communities. Entertaining can be intimidating, however bringing people together does not have to be difficult. Sometimes when I invite people into my home, I ask for each family to bring

a dish to share. Most people want to be able to help, and they want to feel they are contributing. Entertaining in a way in which everyone contributes, benefits both the hosts and guests.

The presentation of the meal, the set table and the flowers, the thankfulness surrounding the meal, the wholesomeness of the meal, and the taste of the meal are all important elements. Incorporating different tastes, such as salty, sweet, sour, and bitter, and different colors and food groups, help to make the meal nourishing. The sense of taste is developed in a healthy way when the wholesomeness of the food, the quality of the food, is emphasized, as well as a variety of tastes presented in a pleasing, reverent way.

Mealtime can be a well-balanced activity, nourishing the body (healthy food), the soul (a loving atmosphere), and the spirit (sharing, offering).

The Bedroom

The bedroom is a space for rest, refreshment, sleeping, and waking. It is a place for indoor play, as well as a place for rest. The bedroom is a place of soft sunlight, gentle evening shadows.

For children, patterns in wallpapers and bedding can be kept to a minimum; solid, harmonious, restful colors are preferable. Very busy wallpaper, while perhaps delightful for grown-ups, can be over-stimulating for children, as they try to process the experience of being surrounded by wallpaper decorated with hundreds of little giraffes and dancing elephants or thousands of miniature trains. Instead of being busy, the bedroom can have a warm, calm atmosphere. The bedding can be made with natural fibers—wool and cotton in soothing colors. Many stuffed animals on the bed can be avoided as too chaotic. Instead, just one stuffed animal or a doll can accompany the child to sleep if he or she wishes.

Bringing color into the home and into the bedroom is an artistic opportunity to influence the mood and beauty of the rooms. Color is one way in which to dress the architectural forms of a home. One painting technique that is useful for creating lively color is called "Lazure." The technique requires painting very dilute, almost transparent layers of color on a white background. The effect is color that reflects into the room. Lazure painting strives for a moving, weightless aspect of color, a color that does not remain fixed. Even if certain painting techniques are not feasible, nontoxic, naturally pigmented paint is readily available.

Toys in the bedroom might include an arrangement of baskets filled with shells, stones, pieces of wood, and other treasures found in nature. Utensils, little dishes, a broom, and other useful daily items are also healthy toys for a child. Items in the bedroom can nurture the senses with delicacy and gentleness. Ideally, children should feel protected and cared for in their bedroom. Toys can be chosen consciously. The sense of touch is developed through the toys with which a child plays. Whether the toys are of natural materials or of plastic affects the child's developing senses.

Our senses are easily stimulated. Through touch we can feel the coolness of metal, the softness of fabric, and the solidity of wood. We sense the difference between a plastic flower and a real one. A plastic flower is merely an approximation of the real thing and doesn't feel, smell, or taste like a genuine flower, nor does it look quite right. Like many plastic objects, it is useful but ultimately disappointing. Plastic toys offer a similar type of experience for the young child. There is an experiential difference between plastic and wooden toys. Playthings made of natural materials ring true to the imagination—sticks and shells and crystals and wool animals and carved wooden boats and pebbles and silk capes.

Children can see how some toys work (the wheels are attached to the body of the car), and there is a difference between those toys

Encouraging children to do things for themselves helps develop their independence and confidence.

At the end of the day, after a child has played hard all day, the bedroom becomes a sanctuary for rest and the rejuvenation of sleep. After the exertion of a day

and electronic toys, which children cannot understand, as they may buzz and light up at random moments. Random and unpredictable experiences cause children to feel insecure and anxious. Noisy and flashy toys can also be over-stimulating for a child. Moreover, young children are highly imitative of their parents, friends, and even toys. Small children can find themselves trapped in a weird kind of play as they try to imitate buzzing and flashing toys.

A child's bedroom can be set up as to be safe for unsupervised play. When children are able to play freely and alone in their room, imagination soars.

of play, physically fatigued, a child returns to the peace of the bedroom to sleep. The bedroom is another place where parents can establish a healthy, daily rhythm for their children. This might occur through regular naps and bedtimes that include a consistent bedtime routine, which might include a story by candlelight, songs, a gentle massage, a prayer.

Bedtime can be a point of much tension for families. The children are tired and falling apart; the parents are tired and impatient—the combination can be disastrous. Establishing a strong and consistent bedtime routine helps reign in the chaos. Our own routine rarely varies: pajamas, bathroom, teeth, and bed. Then I light a beeswax candle, read a book, give my child a massage with massage oil and essential oils, say prayers, sing a lullaby, blow out the candle. Good night! The routine has remained essentially the same for years—completely predictable, no surprises. My children don't

generally complain about going to bed. They love the routine and look forward to enjoying the security and safety of the predictable rhythm every night.

Bedtime can be a good moment to pay conscious attention to a child's angel—giving thanks, asking for help or advice. After

the children have gone to sleep, a parent might return to their room to check on them, fix their covers. This can be a moment to acknowledge the presence of the child's angel. If a parent's task is to help children find their own way, to find their real task in life, then parents can be thankful for the help of the child's angel.

It has been helpful for me to have the feeling that I am not alone in caring for my children. In addition to our family and our community, an angel is also keeping my child safe. I have tried to work with this angel, this spiritual presence in my child's life. At night before bed, I might express a challenge silently to my children's angels, for example: When my children fight, I get so frustrated and I don't

know how to keep them from needling each other without losing my temper. The next time the children are fighting again and the opportunity presents itself, I may find that I am able to meet the situation with renewed imagination and patience on my part, redirecting their attention away from the problem without making the situation worse with my own anger. A good night's sleep, some perspective and consciousness regarding my own behavior, and perhaps the advice of an angel can make all the difference.

For the morning routine, children might wake up on their own at a consistent time, or they might be wakened with a little morning verse or song as the curtains are opened and sunlight enters the room.

A child who is ill can be put to bed in a comforting and restful bedroom. Illness is an opportunity for caring. Essential oils can be used to great effect in the bedroom for both ill and healthy children. A few drops of lavender on a tissue can be tucked into a pillow for a soothing scent and sweet dreams. If someone is suffering with a cold, eucalyptus can help cleanse the air and make it easier to breath. Illness can be a special moment to offer love and attention. Essential oils can be incorporated into caregiving with relative ease and safety.

The bedroom is a place where inner warmth may be cultivated consciously through meditation, attention, and love. In the bedroom, as elsewhere in our home, we seek to nourish a culture of love and harmony. We can seek a calm, reflective, and meditative mood in our bedrooms. The bedroom can be a private and safe place, a refuge of quiet in our busy, noisy lives. A parent's love is a starting point for love according to the classical Greek philosophers. This kind of love encompasses warmth, tenderness, and affection. In Plato's dialogues, Socrates speaks of "training" for love. The parents' love for their children can be a beginning point for that training. Children, with their completely open senses, naturally radiate love and devotion for their parents. Through attention to a child's physical surroundings, toys, and activities, parents can educate children in this initial love and be educated by them in how to love.

A child at the mother's breast listens to the gentle rhythm of her heartbeat. Few experiences are as powerful. Cuddling to a loved one's heart and listening to the beat of the heart, one hears the rhythm of love and affection. A mood of gentleness and softness nourishes this first stage of love, and it is all-encompassing and tender. The bedroom is a natural place to express affection and caring for one another.

Warm and happy relationships fill our homes with love and security. Love between mother and father, parents and children, sisters and brothers fills a home with laughter and peace. Love is not a static activity. Love requires continued effort. If loving is the ability to see the true essence of another, then we must

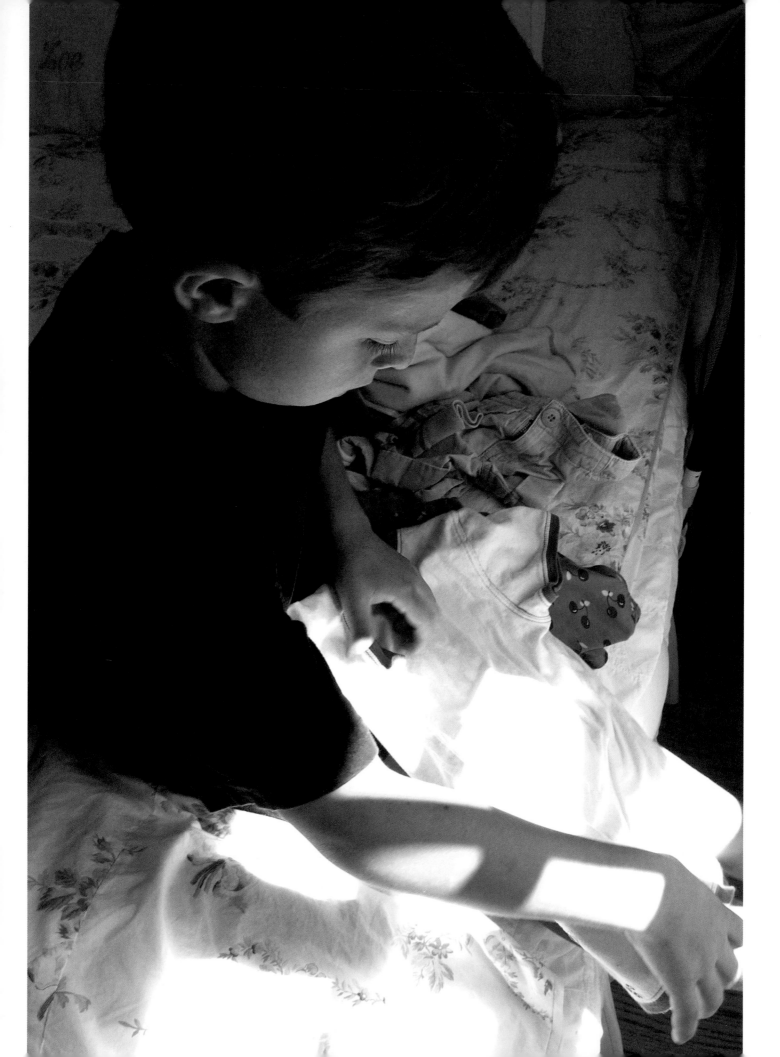

constantly bring that image to mind when others fall short of their true self.

An activity that aids our ability to give the nourishment and the gift of love to another is meditation. Many helpful kinds of meditation exist. One kind of meditation is based on the Buddha's Eightfold Path. The meditations are built around eight themes, each of which can be related to elements of home life. They are:

> **Right commitment**
> **Right self-image**
> **Right communication**
> **Right relationship**
> **Right process**
> **Right initiative**
> **Right learning**
> **Right review**

Parenting and homemaking can be a path of spiritual development, and we can consider these eight themes with an eye to the home and parenting.

Right commitment: Commitment to home and family is sometimes filled with contradictions. I love my children, but I wish I had more time and energy to do the things I used to do before I had children; or I wish I could pursue my dreams that do not include family and home life. How can I renew my commitment and remain committed to my family? Childhood is so short-lived and precious. How can I remain present and committed to my children, living in the present?

Right self-image: We all struggle with vanity and self-loathing. These present a challenge to be clear about who we really are, where our strengths and weaknesses lie. Our children hold up painfully clear mirrors to each of us, exposing our weaknesses.

Right communication: It is important to be clear and honest when we speak with our children and loved ones. And it is easy for misunderstandings to arise in the close living quarters of home. As parents we need to be especially mindful of our speech around small children. Children pick up on every little thing that they hear. My son might be playing on the other side of the house, and if I mention something about a pandemic flu or a plane crash to my husband, I inevitably hear him call out, "What? What are you talking about?" Grown-ups can forget that children are listening to everything said in their presence, even things that aren't meant for their little ears.

Right relationship: Communication, support, and truth are all important components of our relationships with our spouses and children. I often bring my children into my prayers and even into my sleep and dreams by thinking about them before I fall asleep, thinking about the day, about their happy moments and sad moments. I am often moved to apologize silently to them for my haste, impatience, and self-involvement. Contemplating my children helps me to develop a balanced relationship with them, picturing them as they truly are.

Right process: The process of raising healthy children, the process of creating a home, the process of cleaning, and cooking—all these can be examined in our

lives, evaluated and refined.

Right initiative: What is called for by my children? Am I being asked by my children for a certain response to a situation, for new ideas?

Right learning: Am I flexible in my thinking and in my actions, able to learn from my life's circumstances and from my children? Am I involved in learning and studying, expanding and nurturing my abilities?

Right review: Have I given myself the space and time to think about these different areas of my life, to learn and start fresh after reviewing the various aspects presented?

These meditations have been helpful for me (when I remember to do them) in clarifying and pursuing my own development in the midst of caring for house, home, and family. Each day a different theme can be considered.

We all need a place of our own, and if a specific room is not available for solitude and solitary pursuits, the bedroom can also serve that purpose. It can be a place for meditation and reflection, a place to withdraw (at least momentarily) from the busy schedules and from the needs of others.

A quiet space in the day or week can be set aside. Meditation, or even just a moment alone and quiet, can be an important time for parents to renew and refresh their spirit. Parents are often in the situation of giving and giving, while ignoring their own needs. The danger is that we end up feeling empty, with nothing left to give. The bedroom can be a place where we remember to pay attention to our own inner renewal and development.

The Bathroom

For young children, the bathroom is a place of happy splashing, water play. It is a place where children learn to care for their bodies. Most children love their time in the bathroom, to relax in the water, to wonder at the magic of bubbles, to feel clean and safe.

The qualities of water are clarity, transparency, purity, selflessness. We can offer those qualities to our children just by thinking about the various aspects of water when we bathe them. Bath time can be part of our rhythm, a refreshing way to end the day. It offers us as parents an additional opportunity to pay attention to and to care for our children. Surprisingly, it is also possible to have more baths than may be healthy. The child's ability to balance the body's temperature is put to use during bath time; if a child's health is already compromised through colds, the flu, fevers, through over-tiredness or cold weather, then a bath may be too taxing.

I experienced that myself. It was a cold New York winter, and my boys loved their evening bath, a daily dose of water play. However, I found that they were getting sick—a lot. A doctor recommended cutting down on frequent bathing during the winter. I tried it, and they became sick less often.

Bath time offers parents the opportunity to teach children about caring for their own body, brushing their teeth and washing their hands and face. It also

gives children the opportunity to do things for themselves, to be independent and capable.

One can choose healthy and nourishing soaps and cleansers made of essential oils and natural ingredients. Something as simple as washing hands before meals is an opportunity to care in a loving manner for one's children: warm water on a washcloth with a drop of lavender oil can be gently rubbed over the child's little fingers, making hand washing before meals a tender and caring experience. Instead of being a chore, these daily duties can be looked at as opportunities for love and kindness.

Bathrooms can be furnished in ways that are child-friendly. A stool by the sink allows children to be independent in the bathroom. Plenty of towels for drying hands and sopping up spills are help-

ful. A few bath toys—some little fish, a wooden water whistle, some sail boats—can make bathing a happy event.

Essential oils nurture the senses, and bath time offers an opportunity for their use. For children, lavender, Roman chamomile, and Mandarin are among the oils that are safe for little ones. Add just a couple of drops

to a medium such as sweet almond oil or whole milk and swish it around in the water before the children get in.

The sense of touch can be nourished in the bathroom through bathing, through a bedtime massage, through cuddling, through tickling games. Children wake up through touch. It helps children learn their boundaries and become aware of their own body.

Touch is important for children. Parents and educators are seeing an increase in touch-related issues in children—a variety of sensory integration challenges. Parents can greatly affect the physical and mental health of their children by consciously incorporating touch into their daily interaction with them. Touch includes washing a child's hair, rubbing the child dry with a towel. Touch is also roughhousing, swinging a child around (safely), cuddling, skin brushing, and massage.

Over centuries, baths have been known to have restorative powers; it is a form of touch, of sensory stimulation, and a way to bring warmth into body, spirit, and soul. Incorporating a bath into our routines as parents can be very healing. Helpful essential oils include lemon oil for a sunny lift, rosemary for warmth, lavender for cooling and calming.

While the beauty of the home is one area to explore, beauty of body, soul, and spirit is another. The bathroom is often the place to pay attention to our own inner and outer beauty. In some homes the bathroom indeed looks like a shrine or an altar, covered with marble and gleaming silver. We need to nurture ourselves in order to have the inner strength and ability to nurture others. One place in which such self-nurturing can take place is in the privacy of a bathroom.

For adults and children alike, the bathroom can also be a private space. For a mother with young children, it might even be the only place where she can be alone.

The Attic

For many of us, the attic is an important place for storage and for cataloguing and keeping the records of our past. I remember the joys of exploring the attic at my mother's house and at my grandmother's house. The sense of history was palpable among the dusty boxes and forgotten treasures. Hours could pass in the dark and dusty space, the imagination fed by my grandmother's forgotten square dancing crinolines, to be reclaimed for dress-up games, and by the old love letters and high school yearbooks.

In my own attic, I have stored a few items of my past for the adventures of my children. Recently, I was up in the attic with my children to get the luggage down for an imminent trip. They discovered their old booster chairs still being kept for the future use of my young daughter. Down from the attic the booster chairs came, to be used as rocket seats for budding astronauts.

For some, the attic has been transformed into a windowed space, having magical angles and many possibilities. The attic can represent a special place "above the fray." It can be a place for solitude, for removing oneself from the hustle and bustle of the busy life below.

It is important for children (and adults) to have time alone, time when they are not confronted by the critical eyes of others. Children need time when they can play and muse without interruption, without noise, without self-consciousness. Adults and children alike need time to be at peace on their own. We all need the opportunity for inner reflection that solitude brings.

The attic can be an unconventional space and this, in and of itself, can be freeing. The confines of the traditional square or rectangular room can suppress possibility. The tilted walls, softened angles, the more fluid, active form of an attic space can be healthy and invigorating.

In literature the attic is the place where the child flees for safety and privacy, where the adult receives insight and inspiration. It is a place where one can breathe freely, without interference or judgment.

The attic is a secret, private space. This is important in a time so filled with fear, tragedy, and crises, both public and private, and disruptions and disturbances of every sort. An attic is the kind of place where we can release our fears and face the future with courage. The word *respiration* comes from the Latin word *spire*—a word related to spirit, inspiration. In considering the attic, we are reminded of our need to breathe, to expand, and to release the tension of our lives.

The Basement

Beneath the earth, deep and dark, is the basement. The basement often contains the mechanical parts of the home: the plumbing, the laundry room, the workshop with its power tools. It is the working, hidden part of the household.

It is important for children to see people working and to be able to participate in the work. A workshop with its tools and sturdy work surfaces offers children an opportunity to see work taking place and to work side-by-side with a grown-up.

There is a tendency for work to be hidden in today's culture. It often takes place on a computer in an office. This kind of work is too abstract for a child to comprehend. Children need to see their parents, or other adults close to them, working with their hands, with their whole bodies engaged—fixing and making household objects, gluing, hammering, nailing, shaping. Inside and out, up and down, throughout the house, children need to see work taking place in a joyful and fulfilling manner: folding laundry, sweeping floors, raking leaves.

At Grandma's house, the basement contains a wonderful workshop, filled with all sorts of tools and lots of things to be sawed, nailed, bolted, screwed, and stapled. The children love to be down in the shop when Grandpa is working. They love to be working by his side.

The machines of the home—the boiler, the washer and dryer, the water heater and plumbing—are often found in the basement. The working, mechanical, technological aspects of the home are harnessed in the basement. The basement is a great place to work and to learn about how things work.

The Backyard and the Garden

Nature, the outdoors, can provide transformative experiences for children and grown-ups alike. Little can compare to the wide, expansive blue sky, the sturdy tree trunk, sunlight sparkling on the water. All the vistas of the outdoors—from the grandest dramatic mountain cliff and huge crashing waves to the tiniest of wonders, the little ant carrying the snack crumb across the pebbles—  inspire wonder and awe. Most of us have been moved by the sight of the Sun setting and turning the clouds pink, or by the grandeur of mountains rising in the distance. We experience an emotional response that ranges from appreciation to amazement, from gratitude to devotion. By experiencing the wonders of nature, we can learn about the highest form of love, spiritual love—*agape*. It is the love of recognition, healing, devotion, sacrifice. It includes respect and tolerance. The feelings inspired in us by nature teach us about this spiritual love.

Agape arises from the spirit and our inner self. In the home, a parent's deeds and action can be informed by this kind of love. Consciousness can inform parents' actions and they can tend to the children out of these higher ideals, striving toward respect and devotion. The inner work of parents brings this form of love to the children.

Activities of imaginative play, both inside and outside, engage children in body, soul, and spirit. The breathing-out of outdoor play can be contrasted with the breathing-in

of a nap, which also aids the body, soul, and spirit. Both the expansions and the contractions of the day are helpful. Being outside in nature is a vital part of a daily, health-giving rhythm.

Even the scrapes and bumps of healthy outdoor play are beneficial to children. Bumps and scrapes, which cause so many tears, help children to become more aware, more careful, and more conscious. Healthy playground pain teaches children self-possession and restraint. Pain also teaches compassion, because children remember their own suffering when they see another in pain.

Fresh air, sunshine or rain, benefit a child's inner and outer development. Climbing trees, playing in the sand, digging in the dirt, swinging, engaging in all sorts of imaginative and active play help children find their way in the larger world. Movement games, both inside and outside, are important for developing a sense of balance in children. Such activities include climbing, see-saw, jumping, and swinging.

To have a backyard with a swing attached to a tree, some logs to jump on and move about, some bushes to hide under, some flowers to tend—these simple items all aid children in children's development. Such activities both stimulate the imagination and strengthen the muscles.

Yards, back and front, can have rooms as well— places of shelter created by a trellis, an arbor, a gazebo, climbing vines, close-knit trees, a ring of rocks. In our

own front yard are some large bushes. Beneath the branches and leaves is a small enclosed area, a nice little house for the children. A rotting stump under the bushes serves as a table. Little berries are piled up on the table for food.

We have a tree in the backyard that is great for climbing. The children climb up and down the tree all day, enjoying the view from on high.

It is easy to become divorced or distanced from nature and from natural processes. Not all of us live on a farm or in a house with acres of land, animals, and gardens. But sometimes it is possible to have a small garden, to plant some flowers, to work in the earth in such a way that we can demonstrate our connection to it and our gratitude for it.

In our own yards and parks we can reclaim our relationship with nature, and help our children develop one.

There may be nothing more important than for a child to be able to play freely outside, to climb trees, get muddy, jump in water, run barefoot over the grass. This brings joy to children, a joy that will serve them for their entire life. This joy gives children the strength to meet the challenges of life.

Outdoor play is therapeutic and healing. Sliding, swinging, rolling down a hill, playing jump rope— these activities assist all children in finding their place in world, their relationship to the world.

Outside the Home

raveling with young children is tricky at best. Whether it is a trip to the grocery store or the ordeal of an all-day airplane flight, the resulting over-stimulation and exhaustion can lead to tears and tantrums. For the quick errands around town, I try to leave my children at home with a family member or babysitter. If I have to take them, I make sure that I have my shopping list with me to keep things moving quickly. A special treat at the grocery store helps move things along, as does enlisting the children to help gather the groceries.

If we are preparing for an airplane trip, I generally pack a bag with activities for those long hours in the air. The favorite activities of our family include stickers, puzzles, coloring, cat's cradle strings, and games such as tic-tac-toe and magnet checkers. Books and snacks are indispensable, especially small travel-sized books and small snacks. I try to choose low-sugar snacks, because it is hard to manage that extra sugar energy while trapped on a plane. And a few surprises go a long way toward alleviating the inevitable restlessness: a toy they have never seen, a new book, some modeling clay.

For my own part, before a trip I try to be well-rested and calmly prepared for an adventure with an end in sight.

Parenting at Home and Beyond

Being a parent is difficult. Our limitations in meeting the needs or our children are continuously exposed. As a result, it is helpful for parents to practice self-forgiveness. We don't have to worry about being perfect, because it is especially our struggles for love, peace, harmony, beauty, and truth that affect our children. Parenting is a journey, not an end result. Even in our moments of failure, children recognize and benefit from our struggles. As mothers and fathers, we can try to rid ourselves of guilt and find joy with our children. Children thrive on joy and happiness, on laughter and love. For all the mistakes made, we can try to forgive ourselves and bring laughter into our homes.

Today's culture of social isolation, of locked doors and gates, often causes parents to be lonely and to struggle without support. We all need support; we need the support of other mothers and fathers, of friends and families. So, seek out others. Find a group of other parents to meet with— come together for an activity or to play or to share a meal. Seek communication. Seek

encounter. Seek to create a community of love and support for yourself and your children.

Parenting is a fluid activity. It is not a fixed, rigid occupation with one right way and one wrong way. There is no one prescription for creating a nourishing home for our children, for including joy and peace in our lives. There are things that we can do; we can try to pay attention to our surroundings, to be interested in those around us, to be diverse in our interests and activities. We can seek to be nonjudgmental, to meet others with love, to leave others free.

Our homes can be places where children can be children. A place where their trust is met with love and security, a place where they can play unhindered, a place of forgiveness and love, a place of truth and beauty, a place of peace.

The home can be a sanctuary for children. It can be a place that nourishes them, a place that provides children with the strength to meet the challenges of today. Our children can have the opportunity to develop fully, to be loved and to be touched, to be able to move and play, to be able to be both active and at rest in the home and in nature. In this way the home provides our children with the strength they will need to meet the future and to meet the challenges of their lives.

Resources on the Internet

This list represents only a few of the resources available.

Anthroposophy
www.anthroposophy.org

Beeswax Candles
www.bigdipperwaxworks.com

Books
www.steinerbooks.org

Biodynamic Food
www.steinerstorehouse.com
www.biodynamics.com

Childhood Development
www.allianceforchildhood.org

Craft Supplies
www.nearseaorganics.com

Environmental Information
www.ewg.org
www.organicconsumers.org
www.worldchanging.com

Essential Oils
www.jurlique.com

Magazines
www.lilipoh.com
www.mothering.com

Natural Beauty Products
usa.weleda.com
www.truebotanica.com
www.jurlique.com
www.drhauschka.com

Natural Interior and Exterior Paint
www.realmilkpaint.com
www.naturalpaint.com

Toys
www.acorntoyshop.com
www.atoygarden.com
www.novanatural.com

Wool and Silk Clothing
www.nuiorganics.com

Waldorf Education
www.awsna.org
www.wecan.org

Further Reading

Adams, David, *One, Two, Three: A Collection of Songs, Verses, Riddles, and Stories for Children of Grades 1–3*, Fair Oaks, CA: AWSNA, 2002.

Almon, Joan (ed.). *An Overview of the Waldorf Kindergarten*, vol. 1, Silver Spring, MD: The Waldorf Kindergarten Association of North America, 1993.

Bittleson, Adam. *Our Spiritual Companions*, Edinburgh: Floris Books, 2004.

Cohen, Warren Lee. *Baking Bread with Children*, Stroud, UK: Hawthorn Press, 2008.

Cook, Wendy E. *The Biodynamic Food and Cookbook: Real Nutrition that Doesn't Cost the Earth,* London: Clairview Books, 2006.

———. *Foodwise: Understanding What We Eat and How It Affects Us,* London: Clairview Books, 2003.

Dancy, Rahima Baldwin. *You Are Your Child's First Teacher,* Berkeley: Celestial Arts, 2000.

Glöckler, Michaela (ed.). *The Dignity of the Young Child: Care and Training for the First Three Years of Life,* Dornach, Switzerland: Medical Section of the Goetheanum, 2000.

——— & Wolfgang Goebel. *A Guide to Child Health* (3rd ed.), Edinburgh: Floris Books, 2007.

Greenstone, Sandra. *Healing at Home: A Guide to Using Alternative Remedies and Conventional Medicine that Will Change Your Approach to Illness,* Ann Arbor, MI: Healing at Home Resources, 1999.

Hildreth, Lisa. *The Waldorf Kindergarten Snack Book,* Great Barrington, MA: SteinerBooks, 2006.

Howard, Susan (ed.). *The Young Child in the World Today: The Gateway Series One,* Spring Valley, NY: WECAN, 2003.

———. *Working with the Angels: The Young Child and the Spiritual World, The Gateway Series Two,* Spring Valley, NY: WECAN, 2004.

Jaffke, Freya. *Work and Play in Early Childhood,* Floris Books: Edinburgh, 1996.

Jenkinson, Sally. *The Genius of Play: Celebrating the Spirit of Childhood,* Stroud, UK: Hawthorn Press, 2001.

König, Karl. *The Child with Special Needs: Letters and Essays on Curative Education*, Edinburgh: Floris Books, 2009.

———. *The First Three Years of the Child: Walking, Speaking, Thinking*, Edinburgh: Floris Books, 2004.

Kranowitz, Carol Stock. *The Out-of-Sync Child: Recognizing and Coping with Sensory Processing Disorder* (rev.), New York: Penguin, 2005.

———. *The Out-of-Sync Child Has Fun: Activities for Kids with Sensory Processing Disorder* (rev.), New York: Penguin, 2003.

Lockie, Beatrys. *Gardening with Young Children*, Stroud, UK: Hawthorn Press, 2007.

Oppenheimer, Sharifa. *Heaven on Earth: A Handbook for Parents of Young Children*, Great Barrington, MA: SteinerBooks, 2006.

Post, Marsha & Winslow Eliot (eds.). *The Waldorf Book of Breads*, Great Barrington, MA: SteinerBooks, 2009.

Post, Marsha & Andrea Huff (eds.). *The Waldorf School Book of Soups*, Great Barrington, MA: SteinerBooks, 2006.

Schmidt-Brabant, Manfred. *The Spiritual Tasks of the Homemaker*, London: Temple Lodge Publishing, 1996.

Schoorel, Edmond. *The First Seven Years, Physiology of Childhood*, Fair Oaks: Rudolf Steiner College Press, 2004.

Socsman, Albert. *Our Twelve Senses: The Wellspring of the Soul*, Stroud, UK: Hawthorn Press, 1990.

Steiner, Rudolf. *Colour*, London: Rudolf Steiner Press, 2005.

———. *Nutrition: Food, Health, and Spiritual Development*, London: Rudolf Steiner Press. 1991.

van der Ploeg, Inge. *Clear the Clutter: Make Space for Your Life*, Edinburgh: Floris Books, 2004.

van Duin, Veronika. *Homemaking and Personal Development: Meditative Practice for Homemakers*, London: Rudolf Steiner Press, 2008.

———. *Homemaking as a Social Art: Creating a Home for Body, Soul and Spirit*, London: Rudolf Steiner Press 2005.

von Heydebrand, Caroline. *Childhood: A Study of the Growing Child*, Hudson, NY: Anthroposophic Press, 1995.

Wormwood, Valerie Ann. *Aromatherapy for the Healthy Child: More Than 300 Natural, Nontoxic, and Fragrant Essential Oil Blends*, Novato, CA: New World Library, 2000.